# JES
# STORY TELLER

# TOLD BY CARINE MACKENZIE
## ~ ILLUSTRATED BY JEFF ANDERSON ~

COPYRIGHT © 2002 CARINE MACKENZIE
ISBN: 978-1-85792-750-4
REPRINTED 2004, 2009 AND 2015
PUBLISHED BY CHRISTIAN FOCUS PUBLICATIONS
GEANIES HOUSE, FEARN, TAIN, ROSS-SHIRE, IV20 1TW,
SCOTLAND, U.K.
PRINTED IN CHINA

Jesus told lots of good stories.

One day, he told a story about a farmer who was sowing grain in his field. Some seed fell on a path and birds ate it.

Some fell on rocky soil and withered and died.  Some seed was smothered and choked by the weeds.  But some seed fell on good ground and produced a good crop.

Jesus explained the parable.

The seed is like the word of God.  Some people do not understand and Satan snatches the word away.  Others listen joyfully to God's message, but when trouble comes they forget it.

Sometimes people completely ignore what God says – they care more about themselves. But some listen to God's word and understand it and their lives make God happy.

Once, Jesus told an amazing story about a Jew who was on a journey from Jerusalem to Jericho.

All of a sudden he was attacked. Robbers took his clothes and money and left him badly injured by the roadside.

A Jewish priest came along, but he passed
by on the other side of the road. Another
came along. He did not help either.

A Samaritan man then came along. He poured soothing medicine on the injured man's wounds and bandaged them. He put the injured man on his donkey and walked along to the nearest inn.

The next day, he left money with the innkeeper to cover the costs. The Samaritan was the only one who showed love to the injured man.

Then Jesus told a story about a man who had one hundred sheep.

One sheep got lost, so the man left the other ninety-nine sheep and went to search for the missing sheep.

When he found it, he was so happy. Jesus told the people that there is joy in heaven when one lost sinner is found and trusts in Jesus.

'A woman had ten valuable silver coins,'
Jesus said. 'One went missing, so she
lit a lamp and swept the whole house
carefully. When she found it she called her
friends to rejoice with her.'

Jesus then told the people that there is joy like that in heaven when one sinner says sorry to God.

Jesus then told a story about a loving father who had two sons.

One day, the younger one asked for his share of his father's wealth. He left home and wasted all the money.

When his money was done, a famine came to that country. The young man was starving.

He got a job looking after pigs and was so hungry he felt like eating the pigs' food.

One day, he came to his senses. 'I should go home to my father. His servants are better off than this.' He set off for home.

His father saw him coming a long way off
and ran to welcome him. 'Bring out the
best robe. Get him shoes and a ring.'

A big party began. 'My son was lost, but is now found; he was dead, but is alive.' God loves his children like that good father.

Jesus told a story about a man who sent invitations to a great feast, but the guests didn't come. One had bought a field, another some oxen. Another man had just got married. The host was very disappointed.

'Go and invite the beggars, the lame and the blind instead,' the man said.
Those who ignore God's teaching are just like those people who rudely ignored their invitations to the Great Feast.

Two men went to the temple to pray. One was very proud and pleased with himself and he told God this in his prayer.

The other poor man could not even lift up his eyes. He humbly prayed, 'God be merciful to me a sinner.' God was pleased with this prayer.

Jesus told good stories to make it easier for people to understand his teaching. He tells us about God the Father and his love for sinners. God wants us to learn to live to please him.

Matthew 13,  Luke 10,  Luke 15,  Luke 14, Luke 18.